Camp Dream

by Winston White

illustrated by Donna Catanese

Scott Foresman
is an imprint of

Glenview, Illinois • Boston, Massachusetts • Mesa, Arizona
Shoreview, Minnesota • Upper Saddle River, New Jersey

Every effort has been made to secure permission and provide appropriate credit for photographic material. The publisher deeply regrets any omission and pledges to correct errors called to its attention in subsequent editions.

Unless otherwise acknowledged, all photographs are the property of Pearson.

Photo locations denoted as follows: Top (T), Center (C), Bottom (B), Left (L), Right (R), Background (Bkgd)

Illustrations by Donna Catanese

ISBN 13: 978-0-328-39323-7
ISBN 10: 0-328-39323-1

1 2 3 4 5 6 7 8 9 10 V010 17 16 15 14 13 12 11 10 09 08

“I am Miss Jean,” said the camp counselor. “Welcome to Camp Dream.”

Miss Jean and the campers sat by the fire.

"Tell me what you like to do," said Miss Jean.

"I like to cook," said Dean. "I dream of being a great cook one day."

"I can draw!" Sam cried. "I drew this with a lot of colors. I will be a great artist one day. I will have a show with all my drawings."

“I play sports,” said Jess. “I can kick a ball very far. My dream is to be on a great soccer team.”

"Look over here and let's read this sign." said Miss Jean. "How can you reach your dream?"

Becoming an Artist

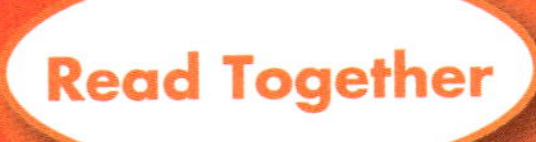

Read Together

Becoming an artist means following your dreams. Tomie dePaola always wanted to write books. He also wanted to draw the pictures for the books. He wrote a lot and drew a lot when he was in school. Now that he is grown up, Tomie writes and draws children's books. You may have read some of his books. One of his books is called *Strega Nona.* Tomie dePaola followed his dreams.

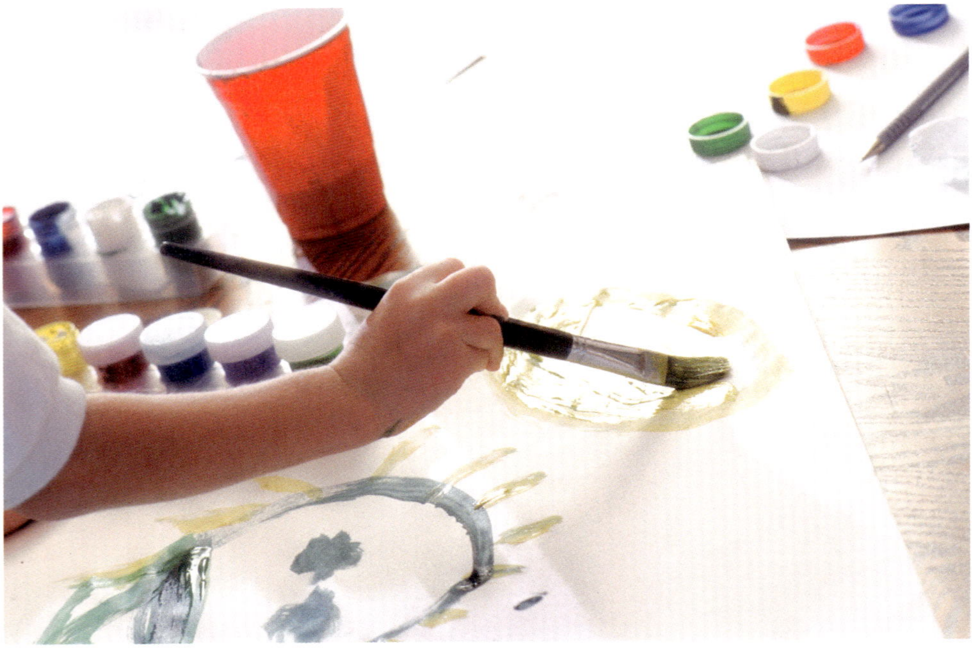